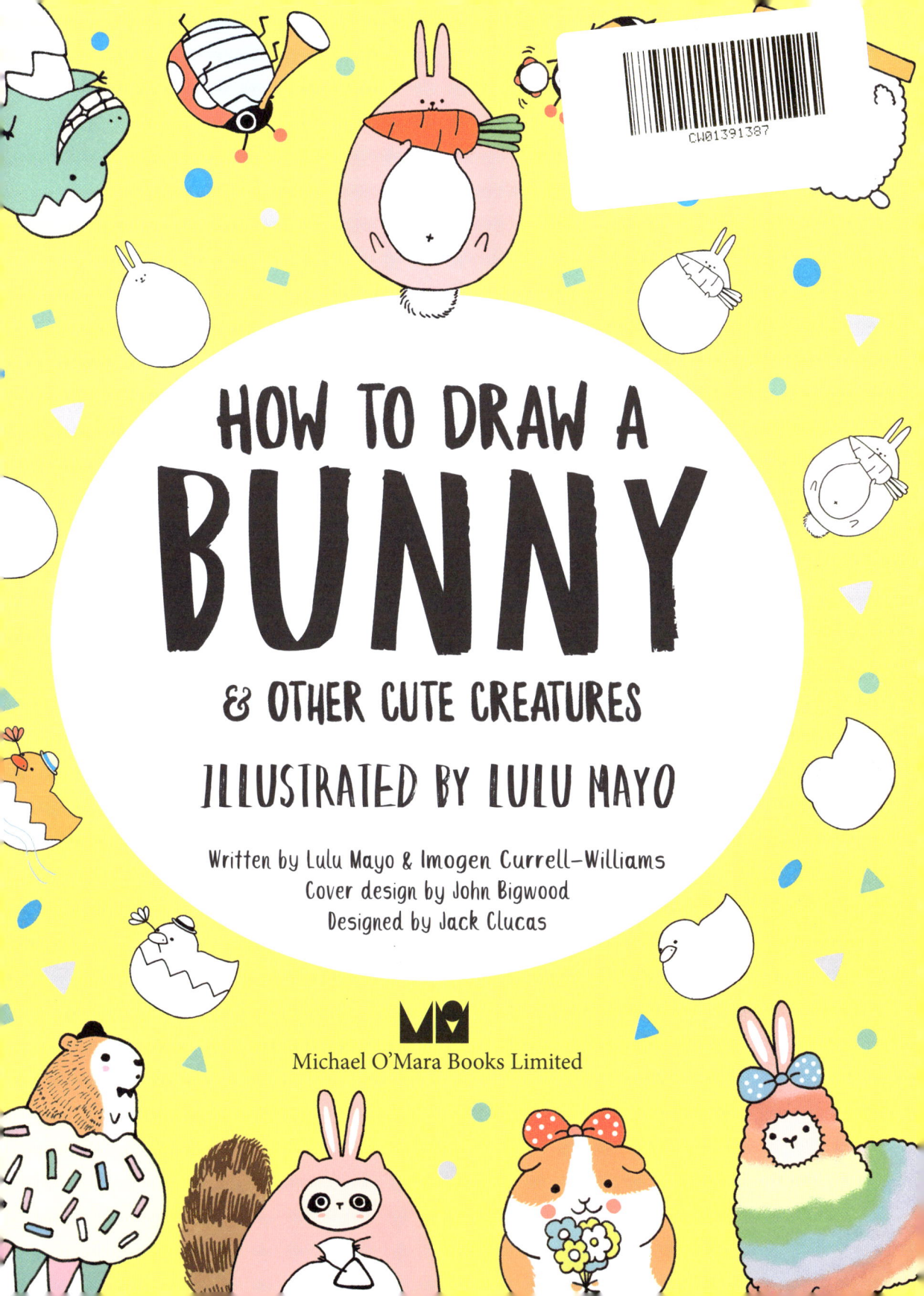

HOW TO DRAW A
BUNNY

& OTHER CUTE CREATURES

ILLUSTRATED BY LULU MAYO

Written by Lulu Mayo & Imogen Currell-Williams
Cover design by John Bigwood
Designed by Jack Clucas

Michael O'Mara Books Limited

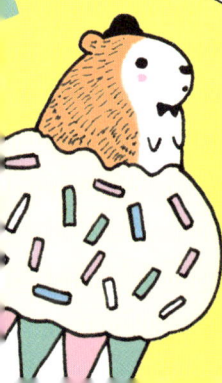

FROM LULU

I hope you love cute critters as much as I do. Inside this book, I'll show you how to draw lots of sweet animals, including guinea pigs, chicks, puppies and, of course, bunnies.

Each adorable creature is brought to life in five simple steps, using shapes that are easy to master. Don't worry if you make a mistake or your pictures look different to mine – all drawings are unique and that's part of what makes them special. Have fun!

LULU MAYO

THE STEPS

The clear, step-by-step instructions for
each creation in this book are easy to follow.

Outlining the body gives
you a great starting point.
Use a pencil to create
your initial drawing.

Add simple detail to
start bringing your
character to life.

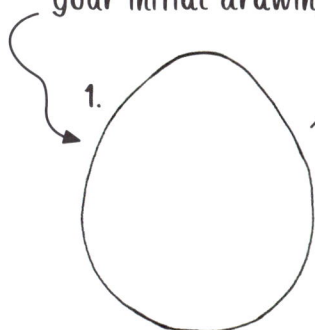

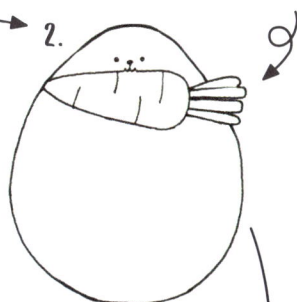

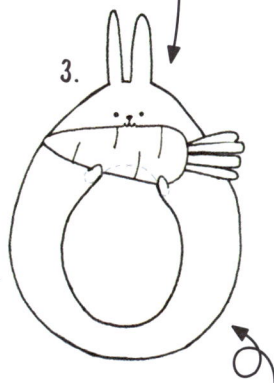

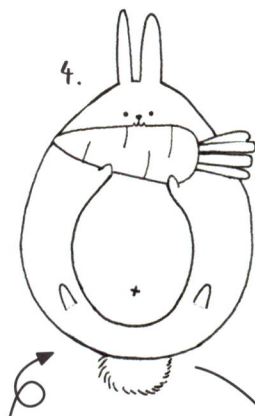

1.

2.

4.

3.

Add extra shapes
& elements.

Rub out the pencil lines
that you don't need.
Then go over the outline
in pen, if you like.

5.

Give it a splash
of colour.

NOW PICK
UP YOUR PENCIL
AND DRAW!

GUINEA PIG

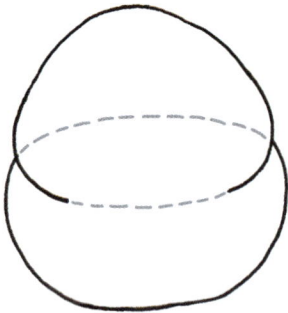

1. ovals for the head & body

2. add eyes, nose, mouth & oval ears

3. add a bunch of flowers & triangle paws

4. big bow & oval feet

5. add markings & a pop of colour

Give it a go here.

Draw more plump guinea pigs here. Try various starting shapes to create different guinea pig poses.

Is it edible, Mr Guinea Pig?

MACARONODILE

1. start with a curved triangle for the face, semi-circle eyes & a spiky triangle body

2. line for the mouth, dots for eyes & nose & rectangles for legs

3. semi-circles & fluffy rectangles make the macaron

4. add triangle spikes on the tail

5. colour your favourite flavour

Now you try.

Time for afternoon tea.
Can you plate up more macarons?

BUNNY

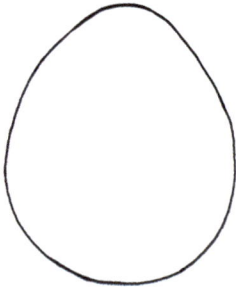

1. egg shape for the body

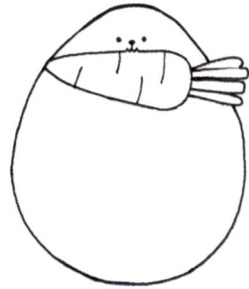

2. add eyes & nose, a triangle for the carrot & rectangles for the stalk

3. long ears & ovals for the belly & paws

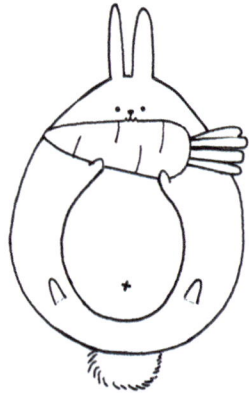

4. triangle legs, a fluffy tail & a belly button

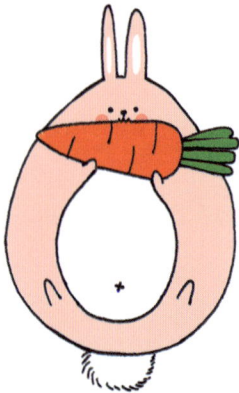

5. give it a splash of colour

Your turn.

Fill the field with cute bunnies. You can
draw them any shape you want.

DEER

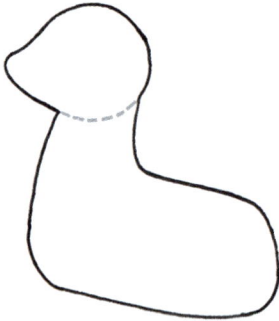

1. teardrop for the head
   & an L-shaped body

2. eye, teardrop ear &
   a heart for the nose

3. triangles for legs

4. add spots & a
   leaf-shaped tail

5. finish with colour

Draw your deer.

Use these shapes to try out different poses.

Come here, deer!

All male deer – apart from the Chinese water deer – have antlers.

DUCKLING

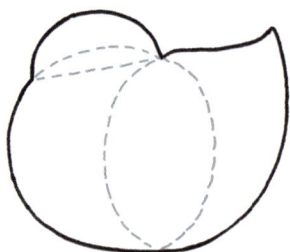

1. semi-circle head, with
a circle & teardrop
for the body

2. draw the beak
& dots for eyes

3. zigzag for the eggshell

4. add a hat & a flower

5. colour it up

Have a go here.

Use these shapes to create your very own duck family.

Bath rubber duck

He doesn't say much.

LADYBIRD

1. eye-shaped face,
a big eye & horn

2. antennae & oval
for the body

3. draw the shell line
& zigzags for legs

4. add spots & belly lines

5. finish with a
flourish of colour

Draw yours.

Fill the page with more lovely ladybirds and clover leaves.

GROUNDHOG MUFFIN

1. ovals for the head & ear & lines for the body

2. add a hat, bow tie, triangles for paws & dots for the face

3. a wobbly oval & rounded rectangle make the muffin

4. draw fur, sprinkles & patterns on the cup

5. colour & decorate

Your turn.

Can you draw a groundhog family peeking out of a muffin,
or a groundhog popping out of another sweet treat?

KOALA

1. oval for the head & fluffy clouds for the ears

2. nose & large dots for the eyes

3. circle for the back

4. chubby triangle arm, oval leg & sausage foot

5. add a flower & colour it up

It's your turn.

Can you complete the scene with more flowers and cute koalas?

Draw a baby
koala here.

LAMB SUSHI

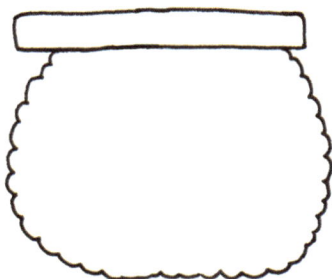

1. start with a
flat rectangle & a
fluffy rectangle

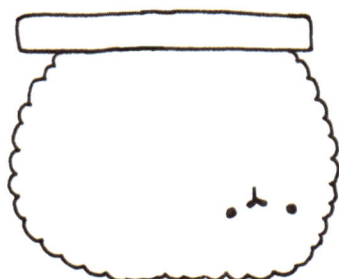

2. add eyes & a nose

3. tall, curved rectangle
& triangle legs

4. oval ears

5. add colour

Try it out.

Use this page to prepare more sushi animals. Or experiment with shapes to create different lamb poses.

Is the hat for me?

CHOCOLATE BUNNY

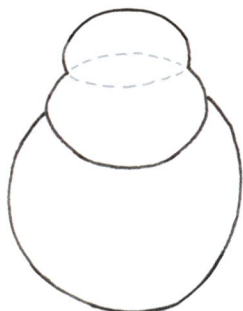

1. two ovals for the head
& a crescent for the body

2. large eyes, nose &
semi-circles for feet

3. ovals for ears
& a flower crown

4. add a bow &
strokes for the fur

5. colour your
chocolate creation

Hop to it!

Create your collection of yummy chocolate bunnies here.

SLOW LORIS

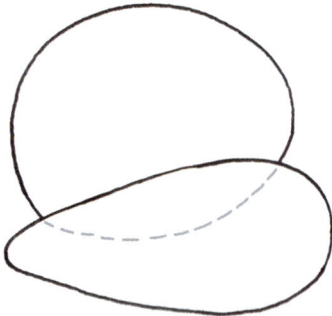

1. carrot shape &
oval for the body

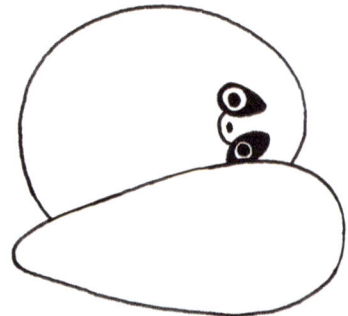

2. draw a cute
facial expression

3. semi-circle ear & chubby
triangle arm & leg

4. add the stalk &
lines on the carrot

5. pick a bold colour

Have a go!

These slow lorises love carrots.
Can you draw more of them having fun?

As they are nocturnal animals,
slow lorises need big eyes
to be able to see at night.

LLAMA BUNNY

1. fluffy, L-shaped body

2. fluffy circle for the face, & dots for the eyes & nose

3. add a bow & ovals to make long bunny ears

4. fluffy triangles for legs & a fluffy oval for the tail

5. add rainbow colours

Give it a go.

Use these shapes to create your own llama band.
Can you draw a llama playing a tambourine?

Shake shake

CATERPILLAR

1. fluffy rectangle

2. dots for the eyes & nose

3. sticks with circles for the antennae & tail

4. triangles for a bow tie & stick legs

5. finish with stripes of colour

Try it out.

Fill this page with more adorable caterpillars.

Do you like
my new shoes?

RACCOON RABBIT

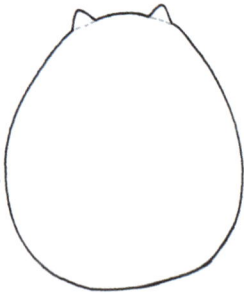

1. oval body & triangle ears

2. heart-shaped face, eyes,
T for the nose & oval bunny ears

3. triangles for the arms &
legs & a circle for the belly

4. add a belly button, a
triangle & a bushy tail

5. add colour to the
raccoon in disguise

Now you try.

Fill the page with squishy raccoons.
How about a dumpling-shaped raccoon?

Yoga
raccoon

Hungry raccoon

Floppy raccoon

BEETLE

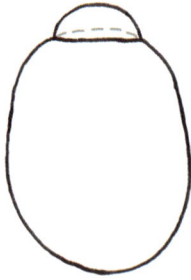

1. semi-circle head &
an oval for the body

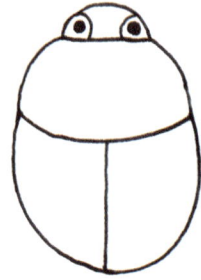

2. big eyes & a T
for the wing case

3. mandibles & antennae

4. add six stick legs

5. dress it up any
way you like

Try it out.

How many different beetles can you draw here?

African
fruit beetle

Hercules
beetle

Stag
beetle

NEST

1. scribble a crescent nest

2. add ovals for eggs

3. a teardrop-shaped body,
fluffy circle for a pompom
& a triangle beak

4. draw the eye, cheek, back
& heart-shaped wing

5. make it bright
& colourful

Your turn.

Help these birds build their home. Draw more birds, nests and trees to complete the scene.

BUMBLEBEE

1. start with an oval
body & a big eye

2. add stripes & antennae

3. a heart for the left wing &
a teardrop for the right wing

4. stick legs, stinger
& a tambourine

5. make it bright
& colourful

Now, you draw one here.

These busy bumblebees are collecting nectar.
Help them by drawing more workmates and flowers.

Can you draw more flowers for me?

DONKEY

1. fluffy oval for hair &
ovals for the head & body

2. add a face
& ovals for ears

3. draw triangles for
legs & add a bow tie

4. add flowers

5. finish with colour

Sketch yours here.

Fill the field with more cute donkeys.

CHICKS IN A BASKET

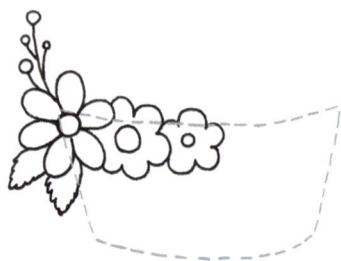

1. start with a rounded rectangle outline for the basket, then add flowers

2. draw fluffy ovals for the chicks, then add eyes, beaks & triangle wings

3. fill in the basket

4. add a semi-circle handle

5. finish with colour

You have a go.

Fill the basket with fluffy chicks. Don't forget to decorate it, too.

Mmm, chocolate.

DORMOUSE

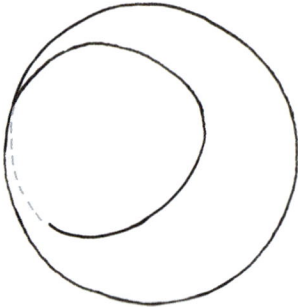

1. start with two circles
for the head & body

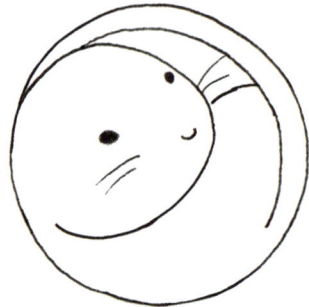

2. draw the eyes, nose, whiskers
& a semi-circle for the tail

3. circles for ears, oval
for arm & two hands

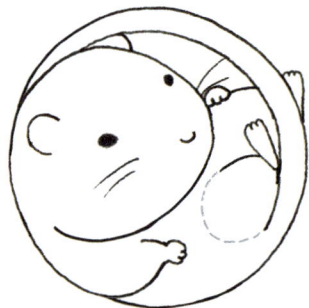

4. oval for leg
& two feet

5. use sketchy colour
to make it fluffy

Your turn.

Use these shapes to create more a-dor-able dormice.

There's no more food. We might as well sleep.

Dormice can sleep for up to seven months a year.

BUNNY CAT

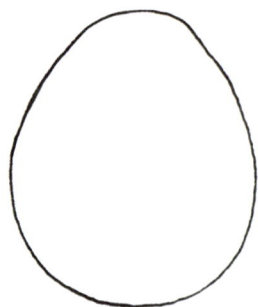

1. oval for the body

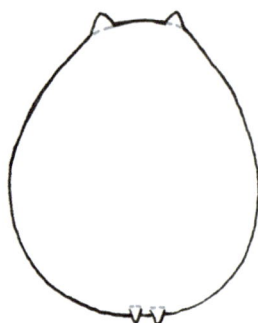

2. triangle ears & legs

3. eyes, nose, whiskers
& a fluffy tail

4. add oval bunny
ears & a bow tie

5. colour it up

Now you try!

Fill the page with fancy kitties. How about a kitty
with a bonnet or a beautiful flower headband?

I've got something
for you.

DINO EGG

1. two ovals for the head,
two lines for the shoulders
& an eggshell hat

2. semi-circle & zigzag
for the shell base

3. add eyes, nose, tummy &
curvy triangle for the mouth

4. rectangles for teeth
& triangle arms

5. a pop of colour & dino's
ready to see the world

Show time!

Create your very own dino egg family here.

CORGI PUPPY

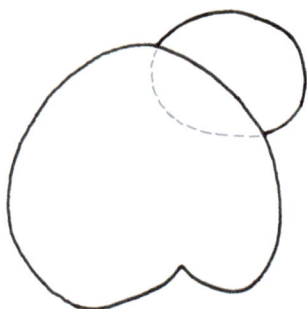

1. oval for the head &
a heart-shaped body

2. eyes, nose, mouth
& triangles for ears

3. fluffy circle for the tail

4. draw a carrot & a bow tie

5. add adorable colour

Sketch yours here.

Fill the page with feisty corgis.

Party time!

BUNNY DOUGHNUT

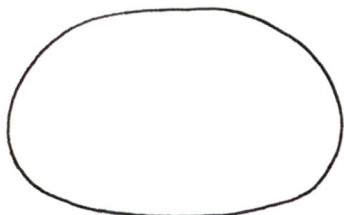

1. long oval for the doughnut

2. ovals for bunny ears

3. eyes, nose & mouth

4. add dripping glaze

5. decorate & colour it up

Draw your doughnut here.

Can you fill the shelves with different flavours of doughnuts?

BABY SEAL

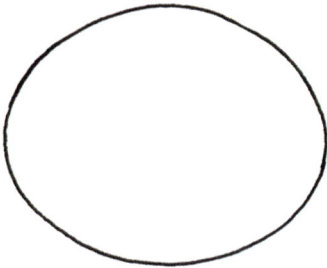

1. oval for the body

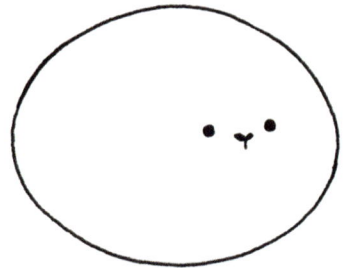

2. add dots for eyes & a heart nose

3. curved line for the chin & semi-circle for the flipper

4. add a bow & hearts for the flipper & tail

5. finish with colour

Sketch a seal here.

Use these shapes to draw more baby seals having fun under the sea.

It's a seal-abration!

BUTTERFLY

1. long, tilted oval
for the body

2. add a big eye & stripes

3. a heart-shaped
wing & antennae

4. draw legs, a
triangle & a stick

5. add a splash of colour

Better try your own butterfly.

Fill the sky with more butterflies.
Add oval wings to create a dragonfly
or triangle wings to make a moth.

UNICORN

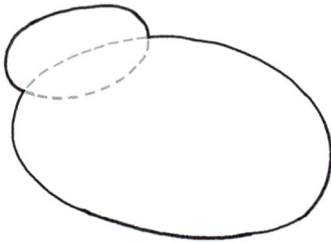

1. ovals for the head & body

2. face, ear, a triangle for the front leg & ovals for the back leg

3. fluffy clouds for the hair & a triangle horn

4. add an egg & a rabbit tail

5. finish with rainbow colours

Your turn.

Doodle some unicorns here. Can you use
the left shape to create a flying unicorn?

CARROT

1. rounded, upside-down triangle for the body

2. add a cute face & triangles for hands

3. rectangles make the stalk

4. add a bow tie & wrinkles

5. finish with colour

Sketch yours here.

Can you grow more carrots in this veg patch?

FLOWER

1. draw a circle with a zigzag at the top

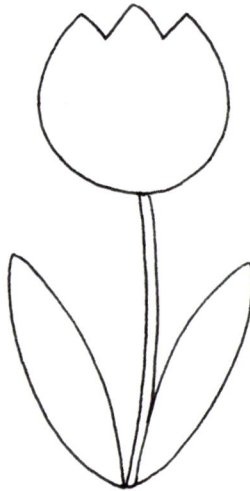

2. long, wavy rectangle for the stem & oval leaves

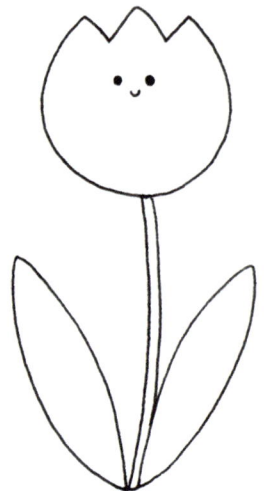

3. add a cute face

4. draw pollen & a pattern

5. add colour – this one's a tulip

Have a go.

Complete the bouquet with your own flowers.
Don't forget to colour it in, too.

SLOTH

1. banana-shaped body

2. triangles for arms

3. heart-shaped face
& a cute expression

4. add claws &
a giant egg

5. decorate the egg
any way you like

Now you try!

Experiment with these shapes to create your own sloths.

Stretchy sloth

Square sloth

Flower-loving sloth

W www.lulumayo.com f @lulumayoart O @lulu_mayo_art

First published in Great Britain in 2021 by Michael O'Mara Books Limited,
9 Lion Yard, Tremadoc Road, London SW4 7NQ

W www.mombooks.com
f Michael O'Mara Books
@OMaraBooks

A CIP catalogue record for this book is available from the British Library.

ISBN: 978-1-78929-294-7

2 4 6 8 10 9 7 5 3 1

This book was printed in China.

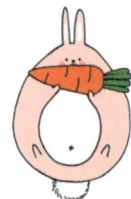